the Soul's agenda

The Soul's agenda

The inner self waits
patiently until we are
ready to discover it

MICHELLE STEVENS

CICO BOOKS

LONDON NEW YORK

Published in 2016 by CICO Books
An imprint of Ryland Peters & Small Ltd
20–21 Jockey's Fields   341 E 116th St
London WC1R 4BW   New York, NY 10029

www.rylandpeters.com

10 9 8 7 6 5 4 3 2 1

A CIP catalog record for this book is available from the
Library of Congress and the British Library.

ISBN: 978-1-78249-337-2

Printed in China

Editor: Marion Paull
Designer: Geoff Borin

Commissioning editor: Kristine Pidkameny
Senior editor: Carmel Edmonds
In-house designer: Fahema Khanam
Art director: Sally Powell
Production manager: Gordana Simakovic
Publishing manager: Penny Craig
Publisher: Cindy Richards

CONTENTS

OPENING

You are not meant to do this alone,
Dear One.

Needing, asking for and accepting help is not a sign of weakness. It is not an indicator of dependence, failure, ignorance, or lack in any way, shape, or form, either. It is actually a sign of great wisdom.

The more you allow yourself to rely on others and on the strength of the whole to heal, create, inspire, and connect, the more in alignment with your source you will be. And the more in alignment with your source that you are, the more powerful we all will be as a result.

So the next time an opportunity arises, Dear One, for you to reach out and ask for help, know that it will be of great benefit to us all for you to take it.

INTRODUCTION

The first time I heard my spirit guides talking to me I was eight years old and on my way to school. When I left the house that morning for my first day in the third grade, I of course had no idea that this was going to be the day I discovered that everything I knew, believed to be true, and had ever been told—as well as everything that those around me knew, believed, and had been told—was not everything that there was to know.

This realization shook me to my core and in an instant changed me forever. The experience itself didn't frighten me, though. It was quite amazing, actually. That first interaction felt as easy, natural, and comforting to me as if my best friend walking beside me had suddenly reached down and taken my hand. But the reality of it all, the realization that nothing was as I believed it to be, terrified me beyond words. In the thirty plus years since then, only two other experiences have triggered that level of fear in me. One was the night when I learned conclusively that suicide was not a way out, and would never relieve my pain. And the other was the time when my father woke me up in the middle of the night to talk, asking for my help because he was afraid, confused, and unsure of where he was, two days after his funeral.

These three experiences were, for me, indisputable examples of spirit stepping into my life and tossing me over the edge of fear, stagnation, and illusion into awareness when I was absolutely committed to not stepping over the edge myself.

Through these experiences, and many others throughout my life, I have been taught, and now believe quite emphatically, that it is not a lack of self-love that is at the root of our suffering, illnesses, addictions, heartaches, self-destructive behaviors, and toxic relationships, but a lack of awareness—awareness of who we are, where we came from, why we are here, what we are capable of, and just how powerful we really are.

I don't believe that we make poor choices because we don't feel love for ourselves or think ourselves unworthy of love. I believe that, in all instances, a love of self is at the heart of all the decisions we make. When we act out, act up, or shut ourselves in to protect ourselves and our sense of self, we do so to maintain the image that we have of ourselves, the identity that we have created for ourselves, at all costs, because we love it and because we love who we are. I truly believe that love of self is not what we are lacking most— it's an awareness of the power of that love that is lacking.

If you knew what I know, if you were aware of the guidance, tools, and support that is available to you at all times, if you knew all that you are capable of and just how powerful you are, if you had an understanding of exactly how to use that power to create, you would be living a very different life. It would not be a life with more love, because you are not lacking love now, but it would be a life of greater ease, filled with more joy, pleasure, and abundance, more of everything that you want for yourself, and less of everything that you do not want.

Like so many others, I experienced a great transformation in my life through illness. With the love, help, support, and advice of my guides, I recovered. However, I didn't heal because they taught me how to love myself. I healed because they taught me what I was capable of, what I could do, be, and become. I healed because they taught me just how powerful I am and how to get in touch with and use all that was available to me. I am still here today because they taught me how to trust, let go, connect, love, heal, create, and inspire. And now, in writing this book, it is my intention to do the same for you by giving you all that I have been given.

It is with great love, excitement, humility, and respect that I share with you the amazing gift that has been shared with me—the gift of awareness.

CHAPTER 1: **TRUST**

How do you begin to trust, Dear One?

Listen to what…

…we are telling you

…your heart is telling you

…your intuition is telling you

…your relationships are telling you

…nature is telling you

…art is telling you

…life is telling you

…and believe it.

When you start paying attention, you will start to notice that all these things are telling you exactly the same story.

Make a conscious decision to shift your attention and not allow yourself to be swayed or influenced by the belief that you know better than all these things. Decide that you are no longer going to allow your mind to hinder your growth using all the cunning, deceptive, and deceitful tactics that the mind uses to do so, such as logic, memory, sight, sound, and perception.

Because the truth is, Dear One, that anything is possible, and possibility is boundless. It has absolutely no limitations. And limitations are, in all instances, nothing more than a product of fearful thinking and an untrusting mind.

When you ask a question of yourself or another, or of spirit, consciousness, or the universe, if the answer that you receive has limits, boundaries, conditions, parameters that you must stay within in order for it to work, you can know for sure, Dear One, you can be certain, that the information you are receiving is not to be trusted.

How do you know what you can trust?

Trust in what you are told if it...

...is loving

...tells you that you can

...points you in the direction of wellbeing

...shows you what is possible

...tells you that you can succeed

...tells you that you can prosper

...encourages you to create

...encourages you to forgive

...inspires compassion

Trust in anything that urges you to connect, feel, see, hear, and experience more joy, happiness, growth, and love in your life. Trust in a source of wellbeing, Dear One. Trust in all that is good, loving, kind, supportive, forgiving, encouraging, inspiring, and nurturing.

Pay attention and learn to recognize the differences between what you can trust and what you cannot, and you will know freedom. You will free yourself from the bonds of unremitting doubt, caution, and fear because you will know, with great clarity, what it is that you really need to be looking out for, and protecting yourself from, and what you do not.

When you can do that, Dear One, and are no longer unnecessarily holding yourself in a perpetual state of preparedness and alert for what may cause you harm or pain, or may deceive you, you will open yourself up to a whole new way of interacting with and experiencing the world. You will then be able to use the majority of your energy on positive, loving, creative endeavors rather than protective ones.

Learn how to trust, Dear One, allow yourself to trust, and you will know at last how it feels to be free. And with that freedom will come an experience of safety unlike any you have ever known before.

Do you think you can do that?

Do you think that you are ready to allow yourself to trust?

ON: KNOWING FOR SURE

• What do you think would happen, Dear One, if you trusted your instincts today totally and completely?

• What do you think would happen if you listened to your heart instead of your head, all day long?

• What do you think your world would look like if you believed yourself to be powerful enough to be the creator of it?

There is only one way to know for sure.

ON: FORGING AHEAD

Why do we want you to trust, let go, and take the leap, Dear One?

There are two reasons:

• So that you know what we already know—that you can do it.

• For the pure pleasure of it.

ON: COMING HOME

It is a glorious thing, Dear One, to walk in your own shoes along a path that you have laid out for yourself.

There is nothing else like it, that feeling of being right where you want to be. It is the perfect fit. It is coming home.

Experience has taught you that when you trust yourself and rely on your inner guidance, intuition, wisdom, and hunches to lead you, you travel in a direction that is conducive to achieving your goals, desires, and wishes. Experience has also taught you that when you ignore your own instincts and blindly follow the advice, guidance, and direction of others, regardless of what your heart is telling you, you end up moving away from those things that you truly want most for yourself.

Chin up—it won't always be a struggle to trust yourself and know which way your heart is leading you. With time, patience, and practice you will learn, and before you know it, the sound of your own heart will be the loudest one in your head.

When you trust yourself enough to let your heart always have the final say before you take action, you will come to know first hand what it means when someone says home is right where you are, home is where the heart is.

Trust yourself, Dear One, connect, and you will be home.

ON: YOUR SHOES

Never mind what you think anyone else would do if they were in your shoes, Dear One.

Never mind what you think they would say or feel, or how they would react, because it will never happen. No one else ever could or will be in your shoes. You are the only one of you that exists and will ever exist.

This is your life. You are meant to experience it any way that you choose.

We hope that this knowledge boosts your confidence in your ability to make the right decisions for yourself.

This does not mean that you should not ask others for their help or opinions. In fact, we believe that doing so is very often a wise and useful thing to do, and we encourage you to do it whenever you feel inspired to do so. There is much that you can learn from the perspective and experiences of others. There is a great deal of benefit to be gained from seeing the world through someone else's eyes.

Just don't forget that their choices, experiences, and decisions are just that—theirs. They were right (or wrong) for them. Learn from them, question them, consider them, but when the time comes for you to make a decision, remember that your opinion, not theirs, is the one that matters most.

You are the world's leading expert on you, Dear One. When you trust yourself, you have very good judgment. Use it.

ON: PROTECTING YOURSELF

Building up your defenses, Dear One, putting up a wall, is one way that you can try to protect yourself from the world.

But you should know that it is far from the best or most effective way to do so.

Cutting yourself off, hiding yourself away, indulging in suspicion, fear, doubt, anger, and defensiveness are all actions that will serve only to weaken you over time. The more you indulge in them, the more they will wear you down, the more disconnected you will feel, and the more vulnerable you will be.

If you really want to protect yourself, Dear One, you've got to do the exact opposite.

You've got to open yourself up, trust, let life in. You've got to make new connections, build up your confidence, and allow yourself to engage joyfully with the world.

If you feel as if you really need protection, build bridges, not walls.

ON: EXCUSES

Be confident. Be present. Be here. Be now.

Trust us when we tell you, Dear One, that there is absolutely no good reason for you not to be.

ON: **WHO TO TRUST**

It is so much more important that you learn to trust and believe in yourself, Dear One, than it is for you to exert a great deal of energy trying to surround yourself with trustworthy souls.

Once you trust yourself—your instincts, hunches, intuition, gut, and ability to read people—you will have little or no need to doubt those around you. You will know whether or not they are worthy of your trust. You will know when they are being truthful or telling you a lie. You will know when their advice has your best interests at heart or their own. You will know these things, Dear One, when you trust the best and most accurate guidance system out there—yourself.

How do you learn to trust in yourself?

You practice, practice, practice. The more you do it, the better you will become at it.

And here is the thing. The more you trust, the more you will attract those who are trustworthy into your life. That's just the way it works.

ON: **HITTING THE WALL**

That wall you've just run into, Dear One, the one that you keep banging your head up against, you should know that it's not actually a wall. It's a door.

And the reason that the door is there is not to keep you out.

It's there for you to open—and it's unlocked.

ON: WHAT TO TRUST IN

*When we ask you to trust, Dear One, many of you ask,
"What is it that you want us to trust in?"*

Well, we will tell you.

We want you to trust in wellbeing, in a universe dominated by wellbeing. We want you to trust that wellbeing is not something that you must work to create for yourself, but something that you must learn to allow for yourself.

We want you to trust that when you let go of negativity, and stop trying to control the outcome of every single experience, situation, and relationship, and when you stop taking a defensive stance against life, that wellbeing, balance, abundance, joy, love, light, laughter, and renewal will rush in to take its place.

That would be a really good place to start.

ON: CHOOSING DIFFERENTLY

*If what you want is more of the same, Dear One, more
of what you've got, keep right on doing, saying, thinking,
behaving, and believing exactly as before.*

But if what you want is something different, you're going to have to trust yourself enough to make the other choice this time.

We know that you know exactly what that is. What we don't know yet is if you're going to allow yourself to choose it. But we can't wait to find out.

ON: WHY TAKE THE RISK?

It only feels as if you are risking something by stepping out into the unknown, Dear One...

...going somewhere that you have never gone before, trying something that you have never tried before. However, the truth is that there is no safer place that you could be than on the edge of something new, in the process of creation.

Resistance causes risk, Dear One. Fear, hesitation, uncertainty, and doubt all serve to pinch off the flow of source energy into your life. Trust, creativity, connection, and creation all serve to open it up. Basically, what we are telling you is that holding back, hesitation, doubt, resistance, and fear are far greater sources of risk for you in your life than trying something new could ever be.

So why take the risk?

Because standing on the edge of something new and being in the process of creation is the safest place that you could ever possibly be.

ON: FEAR VS. INTUITION

How do you know the difference between fear and intuition, Dear One?

How do you know if it is fear that is keeping you from doing, trying, experiencing something new, or if what you are feeling is your intuition telling you that it is a bad idea?

Trust. You trust yourself. That's how you know.

And the only way that you'll ever get any better at trusting yourself, Dear One, is to do it as often as you possibly can.

Oh, and one more thing to remember when trying to discern the difference between the two:

Fear cuts you off from your source.

Intuition connects you to it.

ON: MIND VS. HEART

Your mind knows what it has experienced, Dear One. It knows what it has seen, heard, and been told. Your mind knows what it has touched, tasted, and smelled. Your mind can create great joy, tranquility, and health within you, as well as great distress, turmoil, and disease, with nothing more than a single thought.

Your mind is a very powerful tool.

Your heart knows all, Dear One. It knows eternity. It knows who you are, where you came from, and what you are capable of. It knows that absolutely anything is possible, without exception. It knows more about you than you know about yourself. It is your gateway, your point of connection, to all that is.

Your heart contains the wisdom of the universe.

If we were in your shoes, we would trust our hearts more than we trust logic, our best friend, the Internet, anyone, or anything. If we were you, Dear One, if there were ever a question of which to trust, our heart or our mind, we would choose to trust the wisdom of the heart every time.

ON: YOUR DESTINY

We want you to know, Dear One, that destiny, the universe, God, spirit, prana, fate, life force, serendipity, karma, whatever you want to call it, whatever you believe in, is absolutely, positively, without a doubt, not the most powerful force in the universe dictating the course of your life.

You are.

Believe this to be true, Dear One, and you will be accepting one of the most precious, glorious gifts in all of creation—the limitless power of choice.

ON: THE ANTIDOTE TO FEAR

Clinging to fear when you are in uncertain or unfamiliar circumstances, Dear One, will serve you in much the same way that turning off the water will when you are most in need of a drink.

Fear cuts you off from your source, from wellbeing, and from the guidance, energy, and wisdom that source provides just when you need it the most. Trust in a universe that exists to support you, connects you to your source, and gives you unlimited access to all these things.

Fear cuts you off, and holds you in darkness. Trust opens you up and lets in the light.

The more you allow yourself to trust in the face of fear, Dear One, the more you will be opening up to your source. The more open to your source that you are, the less you will have to be fearful about.

ON: HOW TO STRUGGLE LESS

Trust more—struggle less.

That's all there is to it!

The more you trust, Dear One—your heart, intuition, gut, source, the universe, yourself—the less you will experience struggle.

Don't overthink this one. Don't struggle with the idea or spend too much time trying to decide whether or not you believe this is true.

Just trust that it is, and see for yourself.

ON: ONE AND THE SAME

There is no difference between you and them, Dear One.

You are all exactly the same. It only appears as if there are differences between you because you have all evolved into phenomenal storytellers. The stories that you tell one another and yourselves are so good, so powerful, and so convincing that you, and they, actually believe them to be true and perceive them as real.

But the thing is, they are not. They are just stories.

You are all exactly the same, Dear One.

Can you imagine what your world would look like if you all started treating one another that way?

Try. It's a powerful first step.

ON: SECURITY

Emotional security is a state of mind, Dear One.

The only thing that it requires is you. And you can choose to experience it anytime that you would like.

You can choose to allow yourself to feel it when you have the partner that you want, or the job that you want, or the salary that you want, or the house that you want, or the family that you want, or the body that you want—**or** you can choose to experience it right now, just as you are.

It's totally and completely up to you.

ON: WHAT TO DO NEXT

What should you do next, Dear One?

That depends.

What do you want to experience next?

• Bravery or fear?

• Taking a risk or playing it safe?

• Opening a door or closing one?

• Giving love or withholding it?

• Forgiveness or anger?

• Self-confidence or doubt?

• Patience or frustration?

• Connection or isolation?

• Action or hesitation?

You decide, and then you choose.

So, what's it going to be, Dear One?

What next?

CHAPTER 2: LET GO

You should know, Dear One, that we are not going to tell you that you need to get over it. Letting go has nothing to do with getting over something. And we are not going to tell you that you need to compromise, learn to accept what is, turn the other cheek, embrace the divine, open your heart, be strong, practice compassion, release your anger, or forgive and forget either. Letting go is just not as complicated as all that.

To let go is simply to take responsibility and practice the art of self-love, and nothing more.

How do you do that?

To begin, start by acknowledging your need, your desire, your habitual pattern of wanting to be in control, your belief that it is necessary for you to do something in order to make something happen. Shift into a mindset where you allow yourself to feel, recognize, acknowledge, or even just consider the possibility that sometimes the most productive thing you can do for yourself is not to exert the effort that you think is required to fix things and get things back to the way they were—the way you believe they should be.

Unclench your fist...

...open your hand

...breathe

...love

...and trust in wellbeing.

Allow a desire to feel good—to feel joy, and to be happy, peaceful, and content—to become your priority, at the expense of all other things.

Letting go is not the act of throwing the ball, Dear One; it is the act of releasing your grip on it. Letting go is not about right or wrong, assigning blame or finding forgiveness. It is not about eliminating something, cutting something out, or forcing yourself to move on. It is an act that requires love, not strength, trust not logic, more being and less doing. It is not about making something happen; it is about allowing something to happen. It does not require persistence, brute force, or willpower. It does not leave a hole behind once the deed is done. It does the exact opposite, actually. Letting go is the act of allowing the hole to fill back up. Letting go does not hurt, Dear One; it is relieving. It does not leave you feeling angry or regretful, jealous or sad, rejected or depleted. Letting go is gentle, soothing, healing, and easing. It is the empowering act of loving yourself and it has absolutely nothing whatsoever to do with giving up, giving in, or getting over it.

The most important thing to remember about letting go, Dear One, is that in order to do it, you must first recognize, acknowledge, and accept the fact that whatever it is you are trying to detach yourself from is not holding on to you. You are in fact holding on to it. This point is not debatable. It is not something that is true some of the time, under certain circumstances, for certain people. This is something that is true for everyone, 100 percent of the time. That does not mean that other people cannot, and have not, created undesired or undesirable attachments to you. It simply means that everyone and everything that you find yourself attached to is in that position because of your hold on them, not because of their hold on you.

If you want to let go, Dear One, you are making a powerful acknowledgment that you are ready to take the leap and assume full responsibility for your life.

You are ready to accept the fact that whatever it is you are trying to release is something that, on some level, either consciously or unconsciously, you are exerting energy to remain connected to. If you are able to see that, you will begin to see where and how you are holding on. And once that becomes clear to you, you will be in a position to release it from your life, but not before.

And all you need to do to put all of this into motion is love yourself.

So, are you ready to let go?

ON: **STEPPING INTO THE UNKNOWN**

It is understandable, Dear One, for you to fear change, and to be frightened, nervous, or hesitant about the idea of moving from what is known to what is unknown.

But what if we told you that by moving forward, and embracing change, you would actually be doing the exact opposite? What if we told you that by pursuing your passions, trusting your instincts, taking the leap, and letting change in, you would be stepping back into a very familiar place; a place that is more you than any other place could be, made up of the energy that created you, that you were born into, and that you have spent all of eternity in?

The truth is, Dear One, that the more you trust yourself, let go, and allow yourself to follow your heart, to change and move from what is known to what is unknown, the more at home you will feel, because the more at home you will be.

ON: **IT'S NOT YOUR CHOICE**

Please don't waste any more of your time, Dear One, trying to make the right impression.

Please don't waste any more of your time trying to fit in, to be accepted, or to make somebody see, like, or love you. No matter how hard you try, how much you plan, how much effort you put into it, or how careful you are, you are never going to be able to control what anybody else thinks of you.

That is not your choice to make. It is theirs and theirs alone.

ON: BEING A DISAPPOINTMENT

You are not a disappointment, Dear One.

We are not disappointed in you. We never have been, and we never will be. Ever.

Why?

Because we have no expectations of you. We have only love, acceptance, compassion, support, guidance, and applause for you. We require nothing of you, nothing from you, and we never will. You simply can't let us down.

We don't have a list of rules that we need you to follow or a set of demands that we need you to meet before we will give you our love. It is already yours. All of it. We couldn't love you more than we do right now, even if we tried.

So if that was one of your worries, Dear One, one of your fears, that you were not living up to our, to spirit's, expectations of what you are meant to do, be, have, or accomplish in this life, you can at long last let that one go, once and for all.

ON: LETTING THEM OFF THE HOOK

Release your expectations of them, Dear One.

Let them follow their bliss, and you follow yours. Your happiness is not at all dependent on what they choose to do next. It is solely and completely dependent on what you choose to do next. And you can choose to say, think, or do anything you like.

What more could you possibly want from the moment, from them, yourself, or the universe, than the freedom to choose? And that you've got.

So, are you ready to let them off the hook and start choosing for yourself?

ON: WAITING

Stop waiting for all the right answers, Dear One.

Stop waiting to be certain. Stop waiting for road signs to show you the way. Stop waiting for circumstances to force you into action, or for someone to agree with you or approve of you or encourage you before you take a step, make a change, or take a risk to follow your heart. Stop waiting for permission to live your life. Stop wasting your time waiting.

The time for pretending to be timid, incapable, unworthy, or anything less than you really are is long over.

It's your life, Dear One. You are meant to be enjoying it. There are no rules to follow. There are no right answers. You can't get it wrong. The only person you need permission from to start living the life that you want is you.

So, is the wait over?

ON: FOLLOWING YOUR HEART

If you don't ever trust yourself enough to really let go and follow your heart, Dear One, how do you ever expect to get to where it is trying to lead you?

ON: RETHINKING CHANGE

We know that it can feel as though the act of doing something new—changing your patterns of behavior, thoughts, actions, habits, beliefs, relationships—will require a great deal of effort and struggle for you to achieve, Dear One. But the truth is that movement, progress, and change will always require significantly less effort from you than trying to remain in one place ever will.

As you already know very well from experience, trying to stand still in the constantly flowing river of life requires so much more effort than trusting, letting go, and allowing yourself to go with the flow.

So today, we would like you to consider the possibility that you just may have had it backwards, Dear One—that maybe, just maybe, it is your resistance to change, and not change itself, that is making the process feel so challenging for you.

ON: HONOR

There is no honor, Dear One, in remaining loyal to something that is hurting you—truly, be it a person, an idea, a set of circumstances, a set of beliefs—anything.

We don't want to see you honoring unhealthy, abusive, or painful commitments out of some sense of loyalty or community, or simply to maintain a dynamic that is familiar to you.

We want you to know that we will never see honor in remaining in a bad situation—not in the name of spirit/God/divinity—not because of a promise that you made or a goal that you set for yourself—not even in the name of love, regardless of how strongly you believed in it.

Now is the only time that matters. **Now** is the only moment that really counts. By letting go of unhealthy commitments that are causing you pain, you are freeing up your energy for more worthy pursuits that will serve not only you, but also the greatest good of all.

The universe wants you happy, smiling, content, grateful, joyful, and creative.

Anything that stands in the way of you being all these things is something you can and should let go of. Honor that. Make that the new commitment that you will hold on to, remain loyal to, and never let go of, and let all the others fall away.

ON: DON'T LET GO

If letting go feels too difficult for you, Dear One, if you feel as though you don't know how to do it, are not strong enough or brave enough or certain enough to do it, or if you are afraid of what will happen to you or those around you if you do it, if just the thought of letting go is a source of anxiety or distress, we've got a very simple solution to offer.

Don't. Don't do it. Don't let go.

Instead, focus your energy, attention, and awareness on something else. Focus on something that brings you joy or makes you feel good. Focus on an object of desire, on something that inspires, motivates, and excites you, on something that energizes you, on something that you want more of in your life, not less.

That's it. That's all. That's the solution.

Your attention to something binds it to you, Dear One, attracts it toward you, makes it a part of your reality.

So can you guess what your lack of attention to something will do?

ON: A FRIENDLY REMINDER

In this moment, Dear One, you have the ability to make a different choice, to have a different experience.

You can be brave, take a risk, let it go, love a little more, give a little more, be a little kinder (to them and to you), speak up, trust, try, try again, forgive.

Just a friendly reminder, in case you had forgotten.

ON: FLOATING VS. DROWNING

Expel, release, let go of that which you do not need, Dear One...

...let go of those things that make you feel ill or uneasy, the excesses in your life that are weighing you down, pulling you under. Keep those things that challenge you, enlighten you, brighten your mood, change your perspective, inspire, motivate, and propel you forward. You will know the difference between them by how they make you feel.

You opened up to receive and in the process took a big gulp of water into your lungs. It happens. Don't respond by closing down. Instead, practice opening up to the experience of swimming and not the experience of the water. Do you see the difference? One will cause you to float and the other to drown.

Be kind and forgiving to yourself as you learn.

Don't beat yourself up about what you should or could have done differently, and continue to drown. Allow yourself to move forward from wherever you are with trust, confidence, and faith, and float.

ON: NEEDS

Easy does it, Dear One.

There is no need for you to stress. There is no need for you to take it all on at once—no need to rush through this moment simply to get to the next.

There is no need for you to work without pleasure, hold on to anger, remain fearful, or punish someone else because you are in pain.

There is no need for you to pretend to be someone you are not, or to feel something you do not.

And there is most definitely no need for you to allow other people's circumstances to affect you as much as you have been.

This is your life, Dear One. The most important person in it is you.

The most important moment is now. The most important thing you can do for yourself today is to give yourself permission to re-evaluate your needs.

ON: GIVING UP

Giving up is nothing to feel bad about, Dear One.

Did you know that it's okay to want to give up from time to time? It can actually be good for you. Giving up is the ultimate form of surrender.

When you have nothing left to lose, when you stop trying and stop resisting what is, when you reach your point of surrender, anything can happen, if you let it.

Surrender does not need to be hopeless, devastating, or an indicator of weakness. It can be intentional, exciting, and an indicator of strength. Don't give up and expect the worst. Give up and expect the best. Give up control, fear, remorse, guilt, agitation. Give up negativity. Give yourself a break. Try embracing surrender today and allow something unexpected to happen.

ON: STRENGTHENING YOUR HEART

You don't strengthen your heart in the same way that you strengthen your biceps, Dear One. You don't work it harder to make it stronger. Repetitions of challenging, difficult, painful emotions will not create the desired effect.

The heart thrives on love, Dear One—on compassionate, peaceful, trusting, joyful, loving energy.

If you want to get stronger, if you want to strengthen your heart, don't exert your energy seeking out new ways that will allow you to endure difficult situations, people, emotions, and circumstances for longer periods of time. Seek out new ways to help you to let go of them instead.

ON: SUSTAINABILITY

Do you want to know which of your relationships are sustainable, Dear One, and which are not?

If so, ask yourself this question: At its heart, is the connection based on a foundation of growth, or attachment?

One is sustainable, the other is not. Plain and simple. Do you have your answer now?

P.S. Remember that letting go of the attachment does not necessarily have to mean the end of the relationship. It could be, but it could also be the start of something really great.

ON: CONFLICT RESOLUTION

Just in case you were wondering, Dear One, the antidote to conflict is acceptance—complete and total acceptance—not approval; not agreement; not compromise; not settling; not accommodating; not pretending; not lying; not cheating; not faking it; and most definitely not resignation.

If you want to diffuse a conflict, Dear One, accept what is, exactly as it is, for exactly what it is, as quickly as you possibly can.

Once you stop pushing, resisting, railing against what is, once you let go of the emotional charge that conflict brings to a situation, then, and only then, will you be in a position (a very powerful one, actually) to make a thoughtful, rational, intentional, and heartfelt decision about what you are going to do next.

ON: WHAT YOU CAN AND CANNOT CONTROL

You cannot change the past, Dear One.

You can't undo what has already been done. It's just not possible. It is not within your power to do so.

Isn't that great news?!

You can finally let yourself off the hook and give yourself permission to stop wasting your time, energy, and effort wishing, hoping, and praying that things could have been different.

But what is within your power to change is the way that you feel about an event, circumstance, or experience from your past. In any moment, you can change what it means to you, how you feel about it, its significance in your life, and, most importantly, you can change how you are going to choose to respond to it.

Why not make that moment this one?

ON: FREEDOM

Freedom is a state of mind, Dear One. It is an attitude, a feeling, a way of life.

It is not something that you have to work to achieve or receive permission to attain.

You are free, Dear One...

• to make up your mind about anything, any way that you want

• to change your mind about anything, any time that you want

• to experience the world from any perspective that you choose

We implore you to remember that freedom is a state of mind, an emotion, a lens through which you view your life.

Freedom is not something that is granted by anyone else. It is something that you claim for yourself. You and you alone decide when you are going to choose to believe this, to embrace it, to live it, and to be free.

ON: WHAT MATTERS

We have been asked time and time again, Dear One:

- Does religion matter?

- Does politics matter?

- Does the news matter?

- Does art matter?

- Does their criticism matter? (Or their praise?)

- Does a lie matter?

And every time we are asked, our answer is always the same—we have absolutely no idea at all. It is not for us to say.

But what we *can* say to you with absolute certainty is this:

- Your opinions matter.

- Your ideas matter.

- Your beliefs matter.

- Your actions matter.

- Your feelings matter.

- Your heart matters.

- You matter.

ON: WHAT NEXT?

When in doubt, Dear One, when you don't know what to think, feel, or do next, gratitude is always a really good place to start.

Say thank you for something, anything, in your current reality that is going right, feels okay, and you can appreciate. Let your attention fall fully on what pleases you, holds promise for you, and brings you joy, comfort, or relief—no matter how big or small—and allow all that does not to slip out of your focus for as long as you are able.

And when things that you are not grateful for once again capture your attention, be grateful for your awareness of them and the contrast that they bring, and then once again let them go as you allow your attention to return to being grateful. Repeat as often as is necessary.

Before you are able to take any positive action successfully, which is necessary if you want to generate positive results, you must first be standing in a place where you are able to see things from a positive perspective, where your point of attraction is a positive one. And we can think of no better or quicker way to get you there than with gratitude.

So now back to the question at hand, Dear One—what next?

Our answer to you is that any action taken that is inspired by gratitude will move you in the direction in which you want to be headed.

CHAPTER 3: CONNECT

Imagine if you can, Dear One, having an unlimited supply of love, wisdom, guidance, abundance, and support in your life.

Imagine living every day knowing that all you have done, are doing, and are going to do matters simply because you did it. Imagine never again being without an answer to your question, a solution to your problem; having someone there you can count on and love unconditionally, who will love you unconditionally in return. Imagine knowing that you are not alone, that you are never alone, and that the power that creates worlds is available to you at all times to do with as you please.

Connect with your source, Dear One, and you will no longer have to just imagine it.

A connection to source is not something that can be forced, regardless of how badly you want it or how hard you are willing to work for it. It is not something that can be created through logic, desire, or rational thinking. It is not dependent on your religious or spiritual beliefs, your physical, emotional, or intellectual beliefs, or your past behavior. You do not need to be awake or enlightened, whole or pure, or say, think, do, eat, drink, or smoke anything first in order to connect with the divine.

The ability to connect with source energy is not something that is available only to a select few. There are not some people who are more deserving of it and others who are less. There is no such thing as "more connected" souls and "less connected" souls.

There are no rules in place for how you are supposed to connect, either. You can do so in an infinite number of ways and none is better or worse, more direct, powerful, or effective than any other. Truly.

A connection to source is not something that can be, or needs to be, earned, Dear One. But it is something that can be learned, practiced, and improved upon over time. The sage who has been practicing a spiritual connection for years may be more comfortable, controlled, and confident in his or her practice, but the connection is no more profound, meaningful, powerful, or significant than for the soul who is making a conscious connection for the first time. Every point of connection is divine. Every point of connection is sacred. There is no hierarchy when it comes to alignment with spirit.

Connecting with spirit does not require great effort, quite the opposite, actually.

The more at ease you are, the simpler it will be. Prayers, rituals, traditions, totems, sacred objects, and sacred places can all help the process, but none is required.

You can connect through nature, prayer, a loving relationship, meditation, taking a walk, or any creative act, such as cooking a meal or painting a picture. You can connect through your work, play, pleasure, passion, or even pain. Every creative act affords you the opportunity to connect. All that is required of you to do so is an open mind, an open heart, and a belief that there is more to you, to this life, to this world than meets the eye.

Making the connection is not that hard to do.

You already have the ability, the mechanism, the skill within you to do it well. You are already prepared, Dear One, and more than that, you already know exactly how to find the point of connection within you.

You simply need to remember where it is.

Follow along and we'll help you find it.

What is it that you want most from this moment? What is it that you desire more than anything else? Is it health, wealth, love, security, abundance, beauty, wellbeing, a piece of chocolate cake? Or is it the feeling that you believe having these things is going to bring you? Is it a desire to acquire, achieve, amass, or advance, or a desire to feel connected, to feel as though you are a part of something and that you matter, as if you belong?

If you can understand the difference between wanting something as an end and wanting something as a means to an end, then you can understand where it is within you that you are connected to your source.

The point of connection is that place that feels delight, pleasure, and contentment, that thrill, rush, and exhilaration, that feeling of connection that you experience as joy, peace, satisfaction, safety, and love when you are in alignment. That place that feels safe and comfortable, familiar, and relieving to you. That place that feels like home.

More than anything else, experiencing that point of connection is what you want, Dear One. It is what is driving you, motivating all your actions, behaviors, choices, decisions, and beliefs. Whether you are aware of it or not makes no difference. That desire for connection, that feeling of pure joy, pleasure, and relief you experience when you feel connected to your source, is one of the most powerful driving forces within you.

And here is the best part—you can access it whenever you want, as often as you want, for as long as you want. We are going to show you how.

Are you ready to connect?

ON: A PROMISE

We promise you, Dear One...

- everything will be okay

- you will never be without us

- there is no limit to what is possible for you

- inspiration is divine guidance and following it will never lead you astray

- you will always be beautiful in the eyes of spirit

- you will be loved for all of eternity

- there is always an answer

- you are never trapped

- you can heal from anything

- nothing lasts forever

- if you can imagine it, you can create it

- we always keep our promises

ON: RISE AND SHINE

Rise and shine, Dear One.

There is no need for you to be afraid. There is no need for you to be fearful of the day ahead. We are here with you and we are going to walk this path with you. We are going to take this journey together. We will be with you today, as we are with you every day.

So as you rise, Dear One, keep us close to your heart and know that you are not alone. Know that you are loved, supported, and being guided, and know that you have great wisdom and unlimited creative power at your disposal.

And knowing all this, with great confidence, allow yourself to shine.

ON: IT'S TIME

You are a divine spirit, Dear One.

• You are powerful beyond compare.

• You are a direct channel through which healing flows.

• You are an essential part of all that is:

• Through your thoughts, beliefs, choices, and actions, you are the creator of your world.

And it's time that you stopped pretending to be anything less.

ON: JUST HOW BRIGHT WOULD YOU LIKE IT?

How much light you have in your life, Dear One, how connected you are to source, is entirely up to you.

We—consciousness, guidance, spirit, source—are not more available to you on some days and less so on others. We are not more available to some people and less available to others.

We are equally available to all, like the sun, and from our perspective, there are no rainy days.

The openness of your heart, Dear One, your ability to trust is what determines the amount of light in your life, how connected you are to your source—nothing more and nothing less.

You can choose to open up the shades a little and let in a small amount of light, or you can choose to open them up all the way and let the light pour in all around you.

Just how bright would you like it to be today, Dear One?

ON: WAITING FOR PERMISSION

Don't wait for permission to do what you need to do, Dear One.

Don't wait for someone else to tell you that it's okay to put yourself first. Don't wait until you've got everything else under control before making yourself a priority, before taking care of yourself, before doing what you love.

Those people over there, the happy ones, the rested ones, the ones taking care of themselves, feeling good, enjoying themselves, doing what they love to do, they didn't wait.

And that is the only difference between them and you.

ON: WHERE TO FIND IT

Guidance, source, spirit, light—whatever you wish to call it—is always with you, Dear One, is always available to you.

You are a part of it and it is a part of you. It is within you and around you at all times. You are swimming in it. You came from it and you will return to it.

You can choose not to acknowledge it. You can choose to resist it. You can choose to tell stories that support an illusion of disconnection from it. But you can never be without it.

So if you are looking for it, Dear One, know that you don't have to look far.

ON: LIKE IT OR NOT

Like it or not, Dear One, now is when your life is happening.

Now is when you are at your most powerful. Now is when you can most make a change. Now is when you can make the biggest difference. Now is when your connection with us is the strongest. Now is when anything is possible.

No more waiting, wondering, imagining, or thinking about what your life will be like when…

There is no when; there is no then; there is no later.

There is only now. This is it!

So, what do you think of it? What do you think of your life? Do you like it or not?

If you like it, great!

If you don't, do something about it—not later, not someday, not after, not when…

Now.

ON: YOU'RE SURROUNDED

You are a profoundly powerful, divine spiritual being, Dear One, and you are surrounded each and every day by profoundly powerful, divine spiritual beings.

Some of them may be aware of their divinity, and some of them may not. However, their level of awareness doesn't change who or what they are. The only thing that knowing changes is their personal experience of that truth.

But you can know it, Dear One. You can choose to see and trust and acknowledge their divinity, even if they cannot. While knowing it may not have any impact on them or on their experience of you, you can be sure that it will have a deep and profound impact on your experience of them. And truth be told, that is all we are really concerned with at this time—teaching you, helping you, guiding you toward improving your experience of the world around you and all the people in it.

You are living a life surrounded by spirit, Dear One, steeped in the divine. All you need to do to benefit from this reality is to acknowledge it.

ON: PERFECTION

No one, and we mean absolutely no one, is perfect, Dear One—yet at the same time, you are all absolutely perfect.

This is not just another one of life's contradictions that you are meant to accept. It is simply an answer given from two different vantage points.

From your physical perspective, when you align your thoughts with your physical self, perfection is not possible. People can deceive themselves with an illusion, maintaining a belief that perfection is attainable, but we can assure you that it is not. Preferences are real, Dear One, physical perfection does not exist.

But when you choose to align yourself with your spiritual self, and view the world from a spiritual perspective, then yes, each and every one of you is a perfect soul, a glorious spark of the divine, a piece of all that is.

You are both physical and spiritual at once, Dear One. Don't try so hard to keep these parts of yourself separated from each other. Open yourself up so that you can see, share, and experience both realities simultaneously—your spiritual perfection and your physical imperfections. You are spectacular any way you look at it.

Allow both of these identities to come into focus at once and live your life authentically, auspiciously, and fully awake.

Embrace both your spiritual and physical identities together and you will see a new world emerge before your eyes—boundaries will shift and limitations will disappear.

ON: DISCOVERING YOUR PRIORITIES

Do you know what your priorities are, Dear One?

We are asking you because we think that you might not.

Your priorities are what you spend the majority of your time, energy, and awareness focused on, thinking about, talking about, and doing. For example, you may think your priorities are your health, your wellbeing, your happiness, or your work.

To find out if this is really the case, begin to take notice and ask yourself throughout your day—are you spending the majority of your time thinking about, talking about, and focused on making healthy choices, maintaining balance, feeling good, and creating work that matters? Or are your energy, focus, and awareness directed elsewhere, perhaps on the absence of these things instead?

So, what do you think? Are your priorities where you want them to be, or is a change in order?

The universe is taking its lead from you.

It is prioritizing for you what you are prioritizing for yourself, and is constantly realigning its energies in order to deliver it to you.

So if you are interested in taking full advantage of all the help that is available to you, you may want to take the time to really figure this one out.

ON: DIFFERENT BUT THE SAME

Accepting who you are, Dear One—understanding, trusting, believing that you are energy, consciousness, a divine spirit having a physical experience, an essential part of all that is, connected to everything and everyone, a powerful creator responsible for the expansion of the universe—changes nothing.

• Who you are will remain the same.

• Your face will not change.

• Your gifts and talents will remain exactly as they are.

• Your world will still be round.

• You will still wake up every day in your physical body, and have to tend to your physical needs.

Nothing will be different except your perception of what is, your belief of what can be, your understanding of your connection to all things, your awareness of how you are creating your world, and your experience of everything in it.

Everything will remain exactly the same, Dear One, and nothing will ever be the same again.

Are you ready?

ON: PAUSING

Pause for a moment, Dear One. Be still.

Become aware of:

• your breathing

• your thoughts

• where you are

• your body and how you are holding it right now

• your heartbeat

• how you are feeling

• what it is you want from this moment, and the next

Now that you are aware, Dear One, what is it that you were going to do next?

ON: ASKING FOR HELP

When you come to the realization that you are in need of help, Dear One, ask for it...

...from source, spirit, an angel, a friend, a colleague, your family, a stranger. Just ask. It doesn't matter who you ask, or how you ask—all that matters is that you ask.

Ask for whatever it is that you need. Asking will help you get clear. And the very moment that you do, as soon as you finish asking, start looking for whatever you asked for to show up, because by the time you are done asking, help will already be on its way.

All that remains for you to do after that is to remember to accept it when it gets there.

ON: HOW ARE YOU FEELING?

Pay attention to your feelings, Dear One.

Pay attention to what makes you feel good and what makes you feel bad. Take notes if you have to. Your feelings are communicating very useful, valuable, insightful, powerful, revealing, and actionable knowledge to you all the time.

Your emotions are the language that your heart, soul, and unconscious mind are using to reach out to your conscious self.

Your feelings serve an important function, Dear One. They are speaking to you and telling you something important about yourself, revealing a piece of you to you. They are your heart's, soul's, and unconscious mind's way of asking for your attention, compassion, forgiveness, understanding, love, awareness, and acknowledgment.

They are inviting you to learn and grow, and to have a deeper understanding of yourself. They are providing you with an opportunity to shine a light into the darkness in order to bring awareness, knowing, and consciousness to a place where unconsciousness still lives.

So, now that you know, how are you feeling now, Dear One?

ON: GIFTS

You have been blessed with a great many gifts, Dear One.

We implore you to remember to use them. They serve a far greater purpose than you may realize.

If you are not yet sure what your gifts may be, try answering these questions to help you figure it out:

• What do you do, or what can you do, that brings you joy and connects you with others?

• What do you do, or what can you do, that brings others joy and an opportunity to connect with you, and also with themselves, one another, their community, their bodies, their spirits, their passions, their emotions, and the natural world?

When you discover your answers, you will know what your gifts are.

A gift, Dear One, is anything you are able to do that creates joy and encourages connection in your world.

Your gifts are the channel through which joy and connection are created. Without them, without you, countless joys and connections would never exist. You are the creator of joy and connection in this world, Dear One, and your gifts are the tools of the trade.

So we will say to you once again, you have been blessed with a great many gifts, Dear One. We implore you to remember to use them.

ON: HOW IT'S DONE

Take a moment, Dear One, to feel the beating of your heart. The energy of the universe is powering it, don't you know? It is the vibration, the energy of your spirit that is powering your heart, rushing the blood through your veins, moving the air through your lungs, animating you in this physical reality.

Your soul, your spirit, powers you just as your creative energy powers the world around you. That is why creation is considered a sacred act, Dear One. When you create, when you expel your energy into the world, you are breathing life into it, you are animating the universe, keeping it alive.

Spiritual and physical realities need each other to exist. We power and empower one another. This is how spirit perpetuates itself.

ON: SHOW, DON'T TELL

How would you behave today, Dear One, if you knew that you could do it?

What would you try if you knew that you could accomplish anything you set your mind to? What would you allow yourself to desire if you knew that you were able to attract anything you wanted to into your life? How would you act if you had no doubt whatsoever that you were capable of gracefully and successfully handling anything that came your way?

Don't tell us, Dear One. Show us.

ON: SHARING

Today we have a request for you, Dear One.

We would like to see you share more, to have more open, honest, and genuine shared experiences with those around you. We would like to see you share your true self more—your ideas, thoughts, feelings, laughter, tears, questions, fears, doubts, beliefs, creativity, love, compassion, and so on.

Interact, exchange, contribute, collaborate, merge, network, reach out, unite, keep in touch, correspond, connect, every single chance that you get.

Why?

What happens when you mix two colors together, Dear One? What happens when you mix two ingredients? What happens when you mix musical notes, or numbers, or letters? The answer is that something new happens, something different happens, and more often than not, something beautiful happens.

So now do you understand the reason for our request?

Then get out there and mix it up.

CHAPTER 4: **LOVE**

What a complex word love has become for you, Dear One...

...which is a shame, because the truth is that love is actually one of the simplest forces in the universe. You have come to believe that love is complex because that is what you have been taught, that is the legacy that has been passed on to you. Therefore, that is the meaning you have chosen to assign to the challenges that can accompany the experience of engaging in a loving relationship with yourself or with someone else.

Throughout your life it has been communicated to you in so many ways that love is rare and conditional, that finding it is difficult, and that keeping it requires a great deal of work and adherence to a strict set of rules. Love, you have been led to believe, is something that needs to be proven, proclaimed, and then lived up to. You have come to believe that love has a one-size-fits-all definition that must be adhered to in order for it to be real.

And yet, Dear One, this definition that you have come to know, and come to rely on so ardently, consists mostly of words that describe what love is not— what it does not look like, feel like, sound like, or appear to be. The truth is that there is no universal definition of love. It is not supposed to be defined in the same way by everyone. It is meant to be a unique, very personal experience that is felt, experienced, and shared by you as only you can. The truth, Dear One, is that the only definition of love that matters, or that will ever matter, is your personal definition based on your own experience of it.

Love is not just a word that you say, an emotion that you feel, or an action that you take—it is who and what you are.

It is where you come from and where you will return to. Love is source, Dear One, and an experience of love is an experience of achieving alignment with source.

Acknowledge this, accept this as the truth for yourself, and release all thoughts, beliefs, and judgments to the contrary, and you will open yourself up to an experience of self-love. Do the same for others, see them in alignment with source as powerful, empowered creators, channels of the divine, and you will open yourself up to an experience of truly loving them. What could be more exhilarating, what could feel better, more joyful, meaningful, real, and profound than connecting with another soul and coming into alignment with the divine together, experiencing more of all that is together? Nothing, that's what. That is why the desire to be in love, and the experience of falling in love and being in love, is such a powerful one.

The journey of your life will be a loving one, Dear One, if you spend it coming into alignment with the love that you are while releasing all that you are not along the way.

What could be simpler than that?

You see, Dear One, love is not complex. It is not complicated at all, once you understand what it is and allow yourself to let go of what it is not.

So, are you ready to love?

ON: IT'S NOT THAT COMPLICATED

Matters of the heart, Dear One, always seem to be much more complicated than they actually are.

But, you see, love is love. It is what it is—wonderful, powerful, intoxicating, healing, transformative, transcendent, inspiring, fun. No matter how you slice it, dice it, or serve it up, love is just that—love—and there is nothing complicated about it.

Love only becomes complicated, Dear One, when you begin to put dependencies on it and assign requirements to it, when you decide that it exists only in conjunction with a specific set of circumstances, behaviors, actions, words, or deeds. That is where the complication rests, Dear One—not with love.

The truth is that love has no dependencies and it is everywhere.

You are swimming in it, in fact. All you need to do to experience it is to allow yourself to open up to it—allow it to flow to you, through you, and from you. And the way you can learn how to do that—to open up to the experience of love—is through relationships with people who inspire you to dive in. Through that inspiration you learn to let go, open up, and let it flow.

But remember, Dear One, that love is not sex. And love is not marriage, a family, a promise, a commitment, a duty, an obligation, or a responsibility either.

We want to help you to see that any complications that you think you are experiencing as a result of love are actually a part of your perceived personal reality only, and are not, in fact, a reality of love.

Grant yourself a great gift today, Dear One, and let go of all the rules, requirements, and dependencies that you have put in place as a condition of love. Give yourself permission simply to allow it, experience it, enjoy it, and be inspired by it, transformed by it, healed by it. Swim in it—unfettered, undefined, uncomplicated love.

Life can be complicated, Dear One, but love never is.

Enjoy it.

ON: AN INSIDE JOB

Love is an inside job, Dear One, totally and completely.

Experiencing it, enjoying it, and feeling as though you have enough of it in your life have very little to do with someone else's thoughts, feelings, actions, beliefs, and behavior toward you, and everything to do with your thoughts, feelings, actions, beliefs, and behavior toward yourself.

If you are not open to it, if your heart is not open to receiving love, and if you don't practice loving yourself and others, you will never feel as if you have enough of it in your life, no matter how much someone loves you, how often they tell you so, or how many different ways they try to show you.

But if you are open to it, Dear One—if you open your heart to the experience of love, to the love that exists all around you and is flowing to you and through you at all times—you will never be without it, and you will never know the experience of feeling a lack of it in your life again.

ON: WOULD IT MAKE A DIFFERENCE?

What if, in this moment, Dear One, you decided to love yourself unconditionally...

...to nurture yourself, honor yourself, forgive yourself, care for yourself, prioritize yourself, and accept yourself—exactly where and as you are?

What if, in this moment, you decided to remember that you are worthy...

...that you are divine, and that the reason you are here is to have a joyful experience of being alive?

If you did this, Dear One, would the next choice that you make, answer that you give, action that you take, words that you speak, thought that you think be any different?

ON: DECIDING TO LOVE

Whether or not to love someone is not a decision that can be made logically, Dear One, so stop trying so hard to figure it out. You won't; you can't. Love is not a decision to be made. Love is a feeling, a force, an experience that you allow, share, and enjoy. Either you love, and allow love to flow through you and to you, or you don't.

You allow love, Dear One. You don't choose it. Either someone inspires the feeling and allowing of it in you, or that person does not.

The only decision to be made when it comes to love, Dear One, is whether or not you are brave enough, open enough, and moved enough, and whether you desire a connection enough, to allow, experience, and surrender yourself to it when inspiration should strike.

ON: IS IT LOVE?

The only way to know for sure what love really is, Dear One, is to experience it for yourself.

It is not something that you can learn or come to truly understand from a book, a song, a movie, a poem, or a class.

The best way to have a truly authentic experience of love is to love yourself, purely, totally, completely, and unconditionally. That means thinking, speaking, and acting lovingly toward yourself all the time.

Do that, give yourself the experience of knowing what unconditional love looks, feels, sounds, smells, and tastes like, and you will never again have to ask yourself or anyone else the question, "Is this love?" because you will know.

From firsthand experience, you will then know what true love feels like, so you will be able to recognize if what you are feeling for them is love, and, Dear One, you will know how to recognize if they are truly loving you in return.

ON: YOU'VE GOT NOTHING TO FEAR

Love is nothing to be afraid of, Dear One. Love is not scary. Love cannot hurt you.

It is your worry that it won't be returned, your fear of losing it, your high expectations of it, your perceived lack of it that are causing you to suffer.

Do you want to know how to make all those things go away?

The answer is simple. Love more.

ON: A HELPING HAND

Take notice of the hands that you are holding onto, Dear One, the connections that you are choosing to maintain, and ask yourself:

• Are they holding you up or holding you down?

• Are they pulling you back or pushing you forward?

• Are they leading you in a direction that best serves you or them?

If you are not sure, let go for a little while and find out. It's important that you know.

ON: LOVE

Love is a feeling, an energy, an experience that you open up to and allow to flow through you.

It is a bright light that you shine on an object of desire. It is something that you give away. In its movement through you, love has its strongest impact on you, Dear One. Receiving love is wonderful, but it pales in comparison to the experience of giving it away. Truly.

So when you find someone who inspires feelings of love in you, allow yourself to be moved, motivated, and opened up by it. Don't worry about whether or not you will receive love in return before you begin giving it. Just love. No grand declaration is necessary. No change of relationship status is called for. No long, awkward conversations must first ensue. None of that is necessary for you to give love and have the profound experience of loving. All that is required of you is a willingness to do so. And that, we can see clearly, you've got.

Don't waste time trying to define, understand, or dissect love before you start sharing it. It is not necessary. Just let it flow. Love with your heart wide open and enjoy the experience as it flows through you out into the world, toward your intended and well beyond, without fear, expectation, or hesitation.

Nothing bad ever came from simply loving someone, Dear One.

ON: WHAT'S THE POINT?

The point of seeking out a loving relationship is not to find someone who will love you so that you can have an experience of being loved. You don't need to find someone to love you in order to have love in your life. You are already loved, totally, completely, deeply, and eternally.

The point, Dear One, of seeking out a loving relationship is that it can teach you how to open yourself up to love, to let more love in, to let more love flow to you and through you.

The right relationship will inspire you to open yourself up and allow you to experience more of the love that is already available to you.

Pay attention, Dear One, to how someone makes you feel, to what feelings that person inspires within you. If being in that person's company makes you feel good, if it inspires confidence, bravery, curiosity, kindness, and love, then spend as much time with him or her as you possibly can. But if spending time with them inspires you to feel badly about yourself, and to feel suspicion, insecurity, uncertainty, inequality, and doubt, then regardless of how much love that person claims to have for you, what's the point if the relationship does not allow you to feel it?

ON: WHY LOVE EACH OTHER?

Why should you reach out, open yourself up, be vulnerable, risk rejection, take a chance, cross boundaries, follow your heart, say what you feel, and connect, Dear One?

The answer is simple—because it feels so good to do so.

ON: BEING FOUND

If you want to be surrounded by more people who "get you," Dear One, we'll tell you how to do it.

Don't go in search of them.

Reveal more of yourself, reveal more of who you really are to the world, in all that you do, and they will find you.

ON: PROTECTING YOUR HEART

The best way to take care of your heart, Dear One, to strengthen and protect it, is to open it, trust it, and use it, as often as you possibly can.

Closing it off, shutting it down, or trying to shelter it from unwanted feelings will serve only to weaken it in the end, cutting you off from your source and leaving you far more vulnerable to hurt, deception, and negativity than you would be otherwise.

So the next time you are in a situation where you feel as though your heart needs protecting, remember, there is only one thing that you need to do—open it wider.

ON: MASTERING YOUR HEART

How do you achieve mastery of your own heart, Dear One?

You trust it.

ON: A SECOND OPINION

Your opinion of yourself may change from day to day, Dear One, based on how you feel, how you look, what you think, what you've done (or haven't done), how you loved, what words you used, what you ate, how well you performed, and so on. Some days you will feel that you are more worthy of love, and some days less so. But you should know that no matter what, our opinion of you will never change.

In our eyes, you will always be divine, you will always be sacred, you will always be worthy.

So, the next time you are in doubt and are trying to figure out whether or not you are worthy of love, respect, compassion, or forgiveness, and are in need of a second opinion, please remember to take a minute and ask for ours.

ON: BEING LOVED, CHERISHED, AND ADORED

When it comes to love, Dear One, forget about trying to change, bend, twist, or mold yourself into something that you think will inspire someone else to love you. It is not a worthy use of your time, and it won't work. Trust us.

When it comes to love, what matters most is not someone else's experience of you, but your experience of you.

You want to be loved? You want to be adored? You want to be cherished?

To you we say love yourself, cherish yourself, adore yourself.

The experience of these things will be so much sweeter, and will have so much more meaning, impact, and influence on your life when they come from you than they ever possibly could coming from anyone else. If you don't feel these things or believe that you are worthy of them from yourself first, how could you possibly embrace them coming from someone else?

If you want more of these things in your life, Dear One, give them to yourself. Give yourself all the things that you have been waiting, hoping, and praying that someone else would give to you, and watch what happens. See how quickly others start lining up to give them to you as well—to share in the experience of you with you.

ON: BEING LOVED

You want to be loved, Dear One, and there is absolutely nothing wrong with that.

Everyone wants to feel and know that they are truly loved. You are far from alone in your desire.

But here's the thing about this one particular desire that can make fulfilling it feel so challenging at times—you are already loved, Dear One, truly, deeply, madly, eternally.

• You can choose to believe it, or not.

• You can choose to acknowledge it, or not.

• You can choose to feel it, or not.

That's up to you—but regardless of what you decide, there will never come a time when you are not loved.

Once you believe, accept, know, and trust in it, you will begin to attract more experiences into your life that will reinforce your belief—more people, circumstances, and events that will prove it to you, demonstrate it to you, and help you to experience it more fully.

You can't doubt that you are loved, Dear One, and attract evidence to the contrary at the same time. Trust us and believe that you are, and it won't be long before you forget why you ever doubted it in the first place.

ON: HEAD VS. HEART

Don't fight your heart, Dear One, follow it. There are some battles that are just not worth winning.

ON: MORE THAN ENOUGH

How can you be sure that you will always have enough love in your life, Dear One?

That's easy: love yourself enough. Love yourself totally, completely, and unconditionally. Love everything about you. Love every part of who you are.

We do.

And here's the best part: when you do this, Dear One, when you choose to love yourself enough, then all of the love that others have for you, any amount of love that they are able to shine your way, will be more than enough!

How great is that?

ON: PRIORITIZING YOU

Indulging in feelings of guilt, remorse, or regret for choosing to take care of yourself, Dear One, is like indulging in a hot fudge sundae as a reward for eating less sugar.

You don't need our help to get past this one. What you need is reassurance that it is okay, essential even, for you to make yourself the priority in your own life. And you've got it!

Now the only question that remains is, are you going to grant yourself permission to believe it?

ON: FLIPPING THE SWITCH

Did you know that it takes just as much effort to create a connection to source, Dear One, as it does to lose one?

If you should find yourself in a state of disconnection, please don't be intimidated or discouraged by the effort that you think it will take to reconnect.

The truth is that the only effort that is required is the effort it takes for you to become aware of your state of disconnection and make up your mind to flip the switch back on.

ON: ATTRACTING MORE LOVE

Do you want to know how to attract more love into your life, Dear One?

Love yourself more.

That's how.

Here's why.

The more you open yourself up to the experience of love, the more love you experience, the more love you will attract into your life.

It doesn't matter how the gates of love are opened wider, from the outside or the inside. All that matters is that they are open, wide open, and that they stay that way.

ON: A HEARTFELT REMINDER

The only heart that you have the power to change, Dear One, is your own.

CHAPTER 5: HEAL

You are a part of a larger whole, Dear One.

You are one piece of all that is. You are a spark of the divine, of source, of the energy that created you. You come from the same place that everyone and everything else comes from. Your point of origin is exactly the same as theirs.

When you ignore or forget that connection, when you deny or reject it, or allow yourself to become distanced or disconnected from it, and you can no longer see or feel it within you, a space is left behind where once there was a bond. And that space, Dear One, that blind spot, regardless of how big or small, whether it was created intentionally or unintentionally, consciously or unconsciously, in this lifetime or in a previous incarnation, is in need of healing.

When you come into this world, making the transition from non-physical into physical, who you are—your individual consciousness—inhabits your body. When your soul first emerges into you, it does so with the wisdom, knowledge, and lessons learned from all the past experiences you have accumulated lifetime after lifetime. Your soul remembers them all and carries the memory of them all into you, very much intact. Wisdom, understanding, and experience, once gained, are yours forever, Dear One, for all of eternity, and their keeper is your soul—your consciousness—which are one and the same.

How can you be individual consciousness and a part of the whole at the same time? We'll tell you. Imagine consciousness, the whole, all that is, as a large, exquisitely cut diamond. Each side, each edge, each cut in the stone is unique. It exists in a space all its own, on its own, and contributes to the structure of the whole in a way that no other individual part does or can. And as a result it catches the light and reflects it back out into the world with unprecedented originality. Each unique surface of the stone is a part of the whole, as surely as you are, Dear One, and yet each piece maintains its autonomy because it occupies a space, a perspective, an experience of the whole that is incomparable to any other. Do you understand now, Dear One?

Every point of connection…

…to source

…to your own heart

…to the whole

…is a point that has been healed.

Every experience of letting go, forgiving, loving, and allowing, every choice made compassionately, gracefully, bravely, and joyfully, knowing that you are a part of something larger, divine, and sacred, has healed you. Every point within you that is resistant, every point of separation, disconnection, and denial, every point that does not remember, accept, or acknowledge your connection, is a space that is in need of healing.

Healing and rejuvenation on any level—physically, spiritually, emotionally— are simply the act of reconnecting, letting go of resistance, and allowing your source of wellbeing to be the dominant force in your life. This is a journey of remembering, acknowledging, accepting who and what you really are. And the journey ends, Dear One, when all the wounds have been healed and all the points of disconnection have been mended, and you come to know yourself as a part of the whole, when your individual consciousness, wisdom, understanding, and experiences are once again in alignment with all that is.

You, your soul, has come into this life, Dear One, with a clear and powerful intention to heal, to seek out and experience opportunities for healing.

You have heard us, and many others, say that more than anything else the purpose of this life is to experience as much joy, love, happiness, and pleasure as you possibly can, and that is true. That is why you are here. And the more you are able to heal, Dear One, the more you are able to see, recognize, and acknowledge your points of disconnection and heal them, the happier and more joyful you will be!

So, are you ready to continue on your journey of healing?

ON: THERE'S SOMETHING YOU SHOULD KNOW

You are loved, Dear One...

...beyond words, deeds, thoughts, time, space—beyond compare. We can't even tell you how important it is that you know that.

ON: HOW TO CHANGE DIRECTION

Do you want to know what you can do, Dear One, to start turning things around?

We'll tell you.

Start choosing...

- things that you want over things that you don't want

- activities that you like over activities that you don't like

- people who make you smile over people who don't

- thoughts that make you feel good over thoughts that make you feel bad

That's how.

ON: WHAT IF?

What an enormous waste of your precious time, Dear One, to spend even one more minute wondering "what if?"

Who cares about what could have been? It didn't happen! It wasn't! All of the wondering in the world is never going to change that—ever—regardless of how much of yourself you choose to sacrifice to the idol of regret.

What a shame it would be to miss out on something really fantastically wonderful in the moment because you were wasting your time looking back at your past.

It's time to let go of the disappointment, of the notion that you lost out or missed out on something. You haven't. Trust us. Everything that is meant to be, will be.

Let it go—release yourself from the prison of "what if?" and join us once again in the present moment of "what is." You're the only one who can do it. You are the only one with a key. Use it. We promise you, you won't be sorry that you did.

ON: SACRIFICE

If you want to live a different life, Dear One, the life of your dreams, you can. But you should know that it will come at a cost.

Sacrifices will have to be made.

You are going to have to sacrifice your old vision of yourself—the old story that you have been telling about yourself, the old limitations that you have been holding on to, the old patterns that you have been maintaining, the old heartaches that you have been nursing, the old hurts that you have been honoring.

Do you think you can do that?

ON: AN EMPOWERED APPROACH TO REJECTION

You, Dear One, can choose to approach the subject of rejection in your life in one of two ways:

• You can let "them" and their opinion of you be the determining factor in whether you feel accepted or rejected.

Or...

• You can make a conscious decision to look for, acknowledge, and release old patterns and old feelings of rejection that exist within you, and which you have been either ignoring or holding on to, so that no one will ever be able to trigger them in you again.

Which one sounds like the more empowered choice to you?

ON: BEING PUNISHED

You should know, Dear One, that there is no such thing as divine punishment.

God, spirit, light, chi, prana, life force, source, whatever you choose to call it, does not punish. It does not judge, accuse, blame, denounce, criticize, evaluate, or keep score, either.

It only creates. And you, as consciousness, are the author, artist, architect of all that is created. Life is the canvas, and your choices are the paintbrush through which creation flows.

We will say it again, Dear One, just so that there is absolutely no misunderstanding on the subject:

Punishment is a construct of your own design, and never originates from spirit, ever.

ON: HEALING

Forgive, Dear One—forgive them and yourself. Healing will begin the moment that you do.

Remember, forgiveness is not about condoning, accepting, or dismissing poor behavior, hurtful words, or damaging actions. It is about choosing to prioritize yourself, your health, and your wellbeing over your pain.

ON: CONTRAST

You are not better, worse, taller, shorter, smarter, slower, blonder, balder, funnier, more talented, or more enlightened than anyone in any way that matters or holds any true significance for anyone other than yourself, Dear One.

The contrasts that you perceive in your life every day have true meaning and value only to you. They help you to see clearly what you have more or less of in your life, and what you want more or less of in your life. The more or less has relevance only to you, Dear One, and is in no way a reflection of your worth, value, or stature as an individual, a citizen, or a soul.

You are all of equal value, quality, significance, worth, and height in the eyes of spirit.

ON: A RELATIONSHIP TO-DO LIST

These are just some of the things that you can do for someone you love, Dear One:

- be kind

- be caring

- be complimentary

- be truthful

- be sincere

- be thoughtful in all you say and do

- be compassionate and forgiving

- be honest

- be respectful

- be open-minded

- release expectations

- encourage passions

- acknowledge feelings

- have lots of fun

…and we would like to encourage you to start doing them all a lot more often, for yourself.

ON: PROMISES

Don't allow yourself to become imprisoned by the choices, decisions, and promises that you made yesterday, Dear One.

Your understanding of the world around you is constantly changing and growing. In every moment, the potential exists for you to know something new that you did not know the moment before. This new information is constantly changing your perspective, and this constantly changing perspective is a gift. Don't throw it away simply because you "adamantly" made a decision about something yesterday.

Today, your current vantage point might allow you to see something that will make yesterday's perspective obsolete. Embrace these moments when they happen, Dear One, and allow them to change you, your mind, and your behavior. It would be a real shame to stand in one place all of your life simply because you told someone that you would.

Don't let your desire to be right or loyal or trustworthy supersede your desire to live your life to the fullest.

Don't let the promises that you made yesterday stop you from living your life today. The truth is that the people who you made them to have changed as well. Their needs, desires, and perspectives are not going to be the same forever, either.

Honor yourself and your commitments as they make sense in the moment, and don't allow yourself to be ruled by a past that is already gone or a future that does not yet exist.

ON: **WHAT STAYS AND WHAT GOES**

You decide what stays and what goes in your life, Dear One—you and only you.

You choose what stays by giving your attention to it, and what goes by withdrawing your attention from it.

Give your attention to…

• your insecurity

• the pain in your relationships

• the lack of abundance in your life

• the shortage of opportunities in your work

• all the things that are unwanted in your life

…and they will stay.

So, Dear One, what do you want to see stay and what do you want to see go today?

It's time to choose.

ON: **DEALING WITH ANGER**

If you are angry, Dear One, know this—they are not to blame.

Regardless of anything that they may have said or done to irritate, annoy, or hurt you, they are still not to blame. No one can make you feel something that does not already exist within you. They can inspire you to get in touch with your anger, they can serve as an instigator, their actions can draw your anger up to the surface, but nothing they do can inject anger into your heart.

Isn't that great news?

Now you know, Dear One, that when you are angry and are ready to deal with it, you don't have to deal with them in order to do so. You only have to deal with yourself.

ON: **CHANGING THE PAST**

You want to change your past, Dear One?

You go right on ahead and do it. Don't you dare for one minute believe that you can't.

No, you don't have the ability to go back in time and change the details, the course of events, the physical acts that took place. But what you do have the ability to do is far more powerful than that. You have the ability to redefine them, to change your perspective of them and your relationship to them. You can change what they mean to you, and their significance and importance in your life today.

ON: THE STORM

You don't have to fight the brewing storm, Dear One, or fear it, run from it, or hide from it.

There is another option, you know. You can simply allow it to come, and trust yourself enough to know that you can handle it, whatever it may be.

Truth is, your opinion of it, your feelings about it, your actions toward it, and your awareness of it are all feeding it, adding to it, attracting it toward you.

If you are giving your attention to it, you are contributing to it. So we would like you to choose with great intention what you would like that contribution to be.

You can speed it up or slow it down; make it stronger and fiercer, or kinder and gentler; add levity, compassion, calm, and peacefulness or anger, fear, confusion, and angst. You can even turn it around or stop it altogether if you should choose.

And before you ask, yes, you absolutely are that powerful.

ON: BUILDING STRENGTH

You already know that the best way to build strength in your physical body, Dear One, is to use it. But did you also know that the same goes for building strength in your emotional body as well?

If you want to feel stronger in love, don't wait for more love to come to you, love more. If you want to be more creative, create more. If you want to be more trusting, trust more. Whatever it is you want to strengthen, use it more.

It's just that simple.

ON: THE MECHANICS OF AN APOLOGY

You cannot undo what has been done, change a moment in the past, or take back words once they have been spoken.

You cannot always fix it, Dear One. But you can always apologize.

An apology is meant to serve as a diffuser and an acknowledgment of regret; an opportunity for forgiveness, to allow for the release of the hurt feelings created as a result of a hurtful act, whether it was intentional or not. But before it can have any chance of successfully doing any of these things, you must first forgive yourself for whatever it is you have done.

It is essential that you first release the pain, sorrow, guilt, and regret that you are holding on to.

It is vital that you find a way to let it go, open up, and heal that space within you, so that you can show others how it's done, and have room in your heart to share with them, Dear One, to help give them the strength to do the same.

We understand that what we are asking is not an easy thing to do. But what you are asking them to do is even more difficult than that. How can you even think of asking someone to do this very difficult thing, to accept your apology, to consider forgiveness, Dear One, if you are not willing to do the very difficult work necessary to forgive yourself first?

ON: WHY BE OPTIMISTIC?

Be optimistic today, Dear One.

• Think positively.

• Speak positively.

• Act positively.

Move through your day, believing, trusting, knowing that everything is going to be okay and will work out for the best.

Why?

Because being negative does not serve you in any positive way, and, more importantly, because being negative just doesn't feel good.

Do you really need a better reason than that?

ON: A LIMITED-TIME OFFER

You have a unique opportunity available to you today, Dear One—one that will not be available to you tomorrow.

Today, you have the opportunity to make this day unforgettable.

You can make it the day that you

• risked it all, or played it safe

• finally spoke up, or remained silent

• gave up, or asked for help

• changed your life, or remained the same

This opportunity will not be available to you tomorrow, Dear One. So you had better take advantage of it now, while you still can.

ON: EVOLUTION

You are not here to evolve into a person who is worthy of love, Dear One.

You are already worthy. You were born that way.

You are here to evolve into a person who knows it. And we're here to help you do that.

ON: **WHEN IT HURTS**

When it hurts, Dear One, and you find yourself in a place where you feel battered, bruised, tossed about, and mixed up, remember this. You are not here because you did something wrong, or because you are being punished, tested, or taught a lesson.

You are here because you are being given an opportunity to heal.

Take it.

ON: **NO WORRIES**

You can't worry your way to health, Dear One.

You can't worry your way to success, abundance, joy, security, or love, either. No matter how much of your heart you put into it, no matter how deeply you commit yourself to it, worry is never going to get you to where you want to go.

We are not telling you this to encourage you to ignore your feelings, Dear One. We are telling you this to remind you that focusing your attention on something more productive might just be a much better use of your time.

CHAPTER 6: **CREATE**

You are a powerful creator, Dear One, and you should know that you are never not creating.

From the moment you come into this world until the moment you depart it, you are contributing to the creation of it. When you are sleeping, working, laughing, loving, judging, hating, you are creating.

How exactly are you doing this?

With your thoughts, beliefs, attitude, expectations, imagination, words, and, of course, actions. You are a powerful vibrational being and the energy that you put out into the world has a powerful impact on it, and on you. What you put out there is what you get back. You should know, Dear One, that you are very much in control of the life that you are living. Not only do you have the ability to create for yourself everything that you have been chasing, but you also have the ability to release all that no longer serves you.

There are so many ways for you to do this, so many options available to you for creating the life that you want. While you are deciding which you are going to choose, remember this—the physical act of creation, no matter how precisely, efficiently, or expertly it is performed, will never be more powerful or effective than the creating that you do with an energetic act. Shift your energy, alignment, and attitude, shift your beliefs, expectations, and intentions, and the energy of everything around you will shift as well. All the people, events, and circumstances in your world will be affected in a way and on a scale that could never be generated by a physical act alone.

Everything that affects you, Dear One, good or bad, wanted or unwanted, anticipated or most unexpected, does so because you invited it into your experience, because you allowed it and brought yourself into vibrational alignment with it. Absolutely everything, without exception.

So why, you might ask, would anyone invite tragedy, cruelty, unspeakable acts of violence, pain, illness, distress, or deception into their lives? The simple answer is that, intentionally, nobody would. But intention is not a necessary element in the process of creation. The truth is that most of what people create for themselves they do unconsciously or unintentionally. This is why you are so often surprised, shocked, or feel blindsided when unwanted people, events, and circumstances manifest into your life. The more complicated answer is that there are certain dynamics that you asked to be present in your life before you incarnated. You made these requests, asking for certain people, events, and circumstances to show up to provide you with very specific opportunities for learning, growing, and healing, opportunities that could not be made available to you in any other way. But remember, Dear One, that the importance, meaning, and significance of them in your life will always be determined by you and not by the act itself. What can feel like a tragedy to you may feel like a blessing to someone else.

We are not telling you this so that you will blame yourself for the presence of all that is undesired and undesirable in your life, but rather to excite, inspire, and empower you, to remind you that you are responsible for the creation of your life. By claiming your responsibility, you are claiming your power and making a conscious decision to live your life as the powerful, conscious creator that you are.

So, are you ready to create, Dear One?

Are you ready to move forward consciously, purposefully, and intentionally creating your life?

ON: THE LAWS OF THE UNIVERSE

Today, what we want you to know, Dear One, is that there is absolutely no reason whatsoever for you to fear judgment from us, of any kind.

You can and should feel absolutely free to say, think, and do whatever you like, and to act and behave in any way that you like, in any way that feels good, right, and appropriate to you.

We want you to know that you are not here to learn the rules and follow them. You are here to discover and explore them, and to figure out all that you are capable of doing within them.

The rules, the laws, the guiding principles of creation, of the universe, don't exist to limit you, Dear One.

Their purpose is not to control or manipulate you, or to keep you in line with some master plan—the exact opposite is true, actually. They exist to maximize your potential, your range of motion, and your ability to create. Their purpose is to encourage you to experience all that is possible in this physical reality, and to expand upon it whenever you can. And you never have to worry about breaking them, because you can't.

If some person, book, theory, or concept dictates to you a set of universal rules or laws that do anything other than that, you can know for sure that they most definitely did not originate from the source of creation, the source of all that is.

ON: WHAT'S YOUR STORY?

What's your story, Dear One?

What do you believe to be true about yourself, about others and the world around you, about what's possible? Do you know?

If you are not sure, here is an easy way for you to find out. Stop and take notice. The people, circumstances, and events that surround you are reflecting it back to you, every minute of every day. You are living your beliefs, Dear One. You are living the story you are telling, whether you are conscious of it or not.

If, when you look around, you are not happy with what you see, we would like to suggest that, before you start exerting a great deal of effort trying to change it, you instead put your effort into telling a different story, one that you enjoy and that excites you and makes you happy. Fill it with passages of beauty, balance, abundance, love, health, or whatever else it is that you want more of in your life.

Tell a different story, Dear One, change your beliefs, and let the universe do the bulk of the work for you to bring them to life. Watch as your world transforms around you.

ON: APPROACHING THE DAY

Decide right now, Dear One, before you do anything else, how you are going to approach this day.

Are you going to react to it, and all the people, circumstances, and events in it, or are you going to create it intentionally? Are you going to approach it with confidence or with fear? With trust or with doubt? With excitement or with dread? With self-pity or with gratitude? With an open heart or a closed one? With a belief in limitations or in endless possibilities?

Think carefully about your answer, Dear One. Choose it very consciously, because whatever you decide right now is going to impact every other decision you make, and every single experience you have, all day long.

ON: THE POWER OF RESPONSIBILITY

Yes, with power comes great responsibility, Dear One. But you should know that the opposite is also true—with responsibility comes great power.

The more you take responsibility for your life—your choices, thoughts, words, actions and reactions—and accept that you are the one responsible for every experience that you have, the more powerful you will be.

What we mean by that, Dear One, is the more you are able to accept the fact that life is not simply happening to you, but that you are the one creating it, the greater access you will have to the substantial creative power that exists within you.

ON: WHAT'S WORSE THAN BEING AFRAID

Few things in this world are worse for you, Dear One, or hold more potential for disaster, than moving forward in fear.

That includes doing something that you truly don't believe you are capable of doing or that you don't want to do, as well as doing something that you are afraid to do or that you believe is going to harm you.

Accepting your fears as reality, allowing them to define and restrict you, to tie you up and chain you down to one place, one mindset, one set of limiting beliefs for the rest of your natural life, is one of them.

ON: WHO'S RESPONSIBLE FOR THIS?

Responsibility begins and ends with you, Dear One.

You are responsible for

- the company that you keep

- the work that you do

- the choices that you make

- the actions that you take, and don't take

- your attitude, opinions, and beliefs

- deciding what is and what is not acceptable to you

- when you show up, how long you stay, and when you leave

Just something to keep in mind the next time you find yourself looking around for the responsible party.

ON: DO IT NOW

If feeling better, creating balance, and being happy in this moment were your top priorities, Dear One, what would you be doing right now?

Well…?

What are you waiting for?

ON: STRUGGLING

You have become so accustomed to struggling, Dear One, that you have come to believe that it is a natural, unavoidable part of your life. But we are here to remind you that life is not meant to be a struggle.

Take full responsibility for your choices, all of them, good and bad, let go of anything that does not serve you, and accept what is, and you can put an end to your struggling.

But remember, Dear One, that responsibility and blame are two very different things. Don't blame yourself or others for what is. Struggling persists when you resist what is. Blame is resistant, damaging, accusatory, and segregating. Responsibility is accepting, forgiving, allowing, and inclusive.

When you take responsibility for yourself, your environment, your circumstances, and your choices and stop blaming yourself or anyone else for the place where you now find yourself, you will greatly reduce the amount of struggle in your life, Dear One, and by extension, you will be greatly reducing the amount of struggle in the world as well.

A worthy pursuit, don't you think?

ON: PRACTICING PATIENCE

Learning to play the accordion, paint, teach, or split an atom requires practice, Dear One. So does learning how to be more open, bold, tolerant, loving, trusting, and accepting of yourself and others.

Whenever you are practicing something new, regardless of what it is, we want you to know that it is essential that you remember to practice patience, too, if you ever hope to achieve any level of success.

We are not telling you this so that you will be prepared if whatever you are learning takes a long time, because it may not. We want you to practice patience, Dear One, because of your tendency to judge yourself harshly when you try to do something that you don't yet know how to do. "I can't believe I missed that!" "Why is this so hard for me?" "How stupid am I not to have known that?" You get the idea.

Why does it matter?

Because you can't criticize yourself, be annoyed, or put yourself down, and grow in any positive way at the same time.

ON: BEING LATE

If you are already late, Dear One, rushing, hurrying, being scattered, and stressing out about it is not going to fix it, undo it, or make it better in any way, shape, or form.

But being calm, cool, collected, and fully present when you arrive just might.

ON: COUNTING YOUR BLESSINGS

Why count your blessings, Dear One?

Because when you are counting your blessings, you are not counting your challenges, woes, heartaches, disappointments, fears, pains, mistakes, or losses.

That's why.

ON: BEING PATIENT VS. WAITING

Being patient and waiting are two very different things, Dear One.

Patience is an act of allowing, knowing, and quiet anticipation. It is fluid, changing, and constantly in motion. It is a powerful, empowering, and confident choice that requires your active, conscious participation throughout.

Waiting is a passive, stagnant act, lacking energy, movement, or active participation. It can be frustrating, stressful, and emotionally unpredictable. It is an inert, submissive, and unempowered choice that does not require much of you once the decision to wait has been made.

So when you are in a spot, Dear One, where you think that what happens next is totally and completely out of your hands, think again.

You've still got one more choice to make. And a pretty important one at that.

Are you going to be patient, or are you going to just wait?

ON: MOVING WITH INTENTION

Just as you use your feet to move your physical body in the direction in which you want to travel, Dear One, we would like to encourage you to use your thoughts to move your emotional and spiritual body in much the same way.

If you wanted to go uptown to see a movie, you would not start traveling downtown and assume that if you continued in this direction you would eventually arrive at your destination, would you?

• Do you want to be stronger?

Choose thoughts that make you feel more powerful, not ones that make you doubt yourself and your abilities.

• Do you want to be braver?

Choose thoughts that ground you, not ones that make you feel out of control.

• Do you want to be successful?

Choose thoughts that empower you, not ones that make you feel as if you are incapable.

• Do you want to be desired?

Choose thoughts that make you feel desirable, not ones that make you feel insecure.

• Do you want to feel more connected?

Choose thoughts that bring you closer to your source, not ones that hold you apart from it.

Like your feet, your thoughts are powerful conveyors, Dear One. So why not take full advantage of them? Choose them wisely and with great intention.

ON: TOMORROW

Never stop being amazed by the reality of tomorrow, Dear One, because it is a pretty amazing reality.

The fact that there is a space that exists up ahead of you—empty, blank, full of possibility, just waiting for you to do with it as you please, to fill it up with everything that you desire—should have you over-the-moon excited every single day.

Tomorrow is the space that you leave in your suitcase when you pack for a trip. You leave the extra room because you know that you are going to find wonderful, beautiful, unexpected treasures along the way that you will want to take home with you.

But here's the catch—you must remember to leave room for it. If you pack your bag to the top, if you schedule for and plan out every last detail of your day ahead of time, if you cram your calendar full with the known and predictable, there won't be any space for something new, unexpected, or different to show up— you will be missing out on one of the greatest treasures available to you in this lifetime.

So this evening, Dear One, as you are planning for and anticipating your tomorrow, our recommendation to you is this—get excited and pack lightly.

ON: THE RULES

- Do not be shallow.

- Do not be cruel.

- Do not be offended.

- Do not hate.

- Do not run away.

- Do not hold a grudge.

- Do not tell a lie.

Who made up these rules anyway, Dear One? Was it you? It was certainly not us. Not one of these things is true, you know. You are allowed to indulge in each and every one of them if you choose to do so. But recognize that it is a choice. And whenever you make a choice, we want you to do so consciously and intentionally, ready to take full responsibility for the impact of that choice on yourself, others, and the world around you.

What you put out there is what comes back to you, Dear One. That is a universal law.

Do, be, or say anything you like, but do so with full awareness of the fact that with every choice you make, you are establishing a point of attraction for yourself. You are extending an invitation to the universe to send you back an energetic match.

So, yes, you are allowed to do anything you like, Dear One, but now that you understand the rules, are you sure you still want to?

ON: HAVING A LITTLE FUN

Are you ready to have a little fun today, Dear One?

If your answer is yes, then keep an eye out, because in making that decision you have just triggered a shift in your mind, heart, and body, and in your expectations of the day, and that shift has triggered a shift in your emotions, energy, and spirit, and in the world around you. The universe has already responded by shifting itself to bring you what you want, and as a result, opportunities for fun are already on their way to you!

All that is left for you to do is to remember to choose them when they get here.

If your answer is no, Dear One, it's not too late for you to change your mind.

ON: NOW VS. LATER

If you are waiting for things to get better before you think a better thought, Dear One, you could be waiting a long time. If you think a better thought right now, things would start getting better right now.

So, it looks like you've got a decision to make.

Do you want things to start getting better now or do you want to continue to wait?

ON: CREATIVE WRITING

You are the author of your own story, Dear One. You are the one who decides what kind of story it will be.

So what do you feel like writing about today?

• Adventure, trust, love, compassion, forgiveness, bravery, or perseverance?

• Taking a risk, reaching out, starting a new relationship, or ending an old one?

• Fear, guilt, getting by, playing it safe, or making excuses?

• Jealousy, anger, ego, hatred, frustration, giving up, or giving in?

You've got total creative freedom. Write yourself well!

ON: WITHOUT A DOUBT

We don't doubt, Dear One, not even for a second, your ability to do or be or have or create anything you want— and we never will.

Imagine how different your life, your relationships, your experiences, and your choices would be if you didn't doubt it either.

ON: ONE MORE THING

When you don't have the time, money, energy, resources, strength, or patience to take on one more thing, Dear One, we want you to do just that, take on one more thing—a positive attitude.

It will not cost you a cent, won't take up any more of your time, will not require any extra physical effort on your part, and won't add anything more to your already lengthy to-do list.

It requires so little of you, and delivers so much in return.

We know that you think you have reached your limit, Dear One, that you have taken on all that you can, but trust us, you have not.

Just take on this one more thing, and you'll see what we mean.

ON: SEPARATE BUT EQUAL

There is you, and then there are your thoughts, Dear One.

Both are of equal significance, but they are not one and the same.

So remember that when your thoughts are racing, raging, spinning, tossing, or turning, the rest of you does not need to follow suit.

ON: **WHAT TO DO WHEN YOU REACH THE EDGE**

You know that you have reached your edge, Dear One, when the place where you are standing feels new, foreign, or unfamiliar to you, and maybe even just a little bit scary.

When you come up against it, when you reach your wall, there are a few things that you can choose to do.

You can…

• stop and turn around

• rest comfortably on it

• slowly inch yourself over it

• confidently walk through it

• break it down with thunderous applause

There is no right answer, only a choice to be made. And the choice, of course, is entirely yours. But we are here to tell you that breaking it down with thunderous applause is a whole lot more fun than advancing with quiet confidence—and both are preferable to standing still or moving backward.

Do it your way, Dear One, not anyone else's.

Don't look to others for answers, acceptable protocols, or codes of behavior to show you how you should proceed. The truth is that you are never going to find any that will serve you better than the ones you create for yourself.

CHAPTER 7: INSPIRE

Inspiration, Dear One, is the sensation, the act, the experience of opening yourself up to your source, more than before.

It is the opening of the window, the door, the floodgates, the smallest crack in your armor, opening wider to let in something new and different that would not or could not fit in before—more light, energy, wellbeing, more confidence, creativity, forgiveness, more compassion, love, life, more of who you really are.

To be inspired is to allow yourself to be opened up, stretched, expanded, widened, and moved in such a way as to allow a new path, new possibilities, new options to be revealed to you. Options that in all likelihood have been there all along but that you simply could not see because of your current vantage point, mindset, or habitual belief system. To be inspired is to allow more consciousness, more source to flow to you and through you. That is why it feels so good, Dear One.

You are letting in more of that which you came from…

…more wellbeing

…love   …joy

…creativity

…possibility

…positive energy

…more pure potential than you ever have before.

Sources of inspiration are everywhere—you are surrounded by them all the time. Any place, anything, anyone can serve as a catalyst to help you to open up so that more of that energy can reach you. Let life inspire you, Dear One. Let it stretch you and bend you and turn you this way and that. Let it stand you on your head and change your perspective. Don't fear the unknown when you come up against it; take advantage of it. Trust it, embrace it, let it change you. Take the bait and let it carry you away. It's the only way you'll ever get to somewhere new. It's the only way you will ever grow. The more you allow yourself to be inspired, Dear One, and are able to look beyond what you know, and focus your attention on creating what you want and on what could be, the more you will be serving as a source of inspiration for others, showing them the path to somewhere new, giving them permission to follow it.

To be inspired is to be opened up. To inspire is to serve as a catalyst for opening up others, and the best way to do that, Dear One, is to be yourself, be authentic, brave, daring, curious, trusting, willing to keep putting one foot in front of the other with an open heart and an open mind.

Dance, Dear One, and you will inspire others to do the same.

Inspiration is the cool breeze blowing in through the window on a hot day, and warm water cascading down your back on a cold one. It is relieving, energizing, grounding, and exciting. It is feeling that you are right where you are meant to be, exactly when you are meant to be there. There is no other feeling quite like it—opening up to something you have never experienced before, something completely new and powerful. And we want you to have that experience, Dear One, and to inspire it in others, as often as you possibly can.

So, are you ready to be opened up, Dear One? Are you ready to inspire and to be inspired?

ON: **WHY YOU ARE HERE**

- You are not here to find "The One," Dear One. You are here to know true love.

- You are not here to win awards. You are here to create, bravely, confidently, authentically, and from the heart.

- You are not here to accumulate wealth. You are here to have an experience of abundance.

- You are not here to achieve notoriety. You are here to learn just how powerful, creative, and capable you really are.

Are you starting to get the idea?

ON: **A LIFE OF SERVICE**

The more creative you are, Dear One, and the more you trust yourself, follow your heart, and allow yourself to color outside the lines, the more you will be living a life that is of service to life itself.

ON: DOING YOUR PART

The world has more kindness in it when you are kind, Dear One. It has more compassion when you are compassionate, more love when you are loving, more tolerance when you are tolerant, more hatred when you hate, and more judgment when you judge.

What do you think the world needs more of today?

Are you willing to do your part to see that it gets it?

ON: HOW TO SUCCEED

An artist who is painting, writing, sculpting, composing, inventing, sketching, and designing can make no wrong move. They can make no wrong choice in the creation of their work because it is theirs. It can be big or small, round or square, red or blue. It doesn't matter.

There is no "right" answer when it comes to creating art. There is only preference.

The same is true of life, Dear One—there is no "right" answer when it comes to living your life. Regardless of your vocation, education, skills, experience, sense of color and style, and ability to carry a tune, you are an artist and your world, the reality that you perceive, is your canvas.

Today, we are going to encourage you to add to it. Paint, sing, dance, write, love, laugh, speak up, contribute, and experience every chance that you get, knowing that you can't get it wrong, and that you can't fail.

From our perspective, as long as you are creating and adding to the picture in some way, you are succeeding. You are doing what you have come here to do.

ON: SOLIDARITY

You are under no obligation, Dear One, to take on or share the worries of those around you, in your home, your community, your nation, or the world.

Doing so is not a sign of love, respect, or support. It is not the mark of a good friend, neighbor, or citizen. We will even go so far as to say that if your intention is to do some good, you should definitely not take on their worries or share in them.

In fact, if worry is the only contribution you feel you can make to a situation, you will be doing everyone involved a far greater service by keeping your distance. Adding more worry will not help to resolve anything. It will not contribute in any way to a solution or bring comfort or relief to any of the parties involved.

If you want to be of service, supportive, and useful, and to make a positive contribution, bring something else. Bring hope, joy, a positive outlook, inspiration, motivation, homemade lasagna. Bring anything that you think will help to shift the energy of the group from a negative point of attraction to a positive one.

ON: ACCEPTING YOUR MISSION

Do you want to know what your mission is in this life, Dear One?

We'll tell you.

It is to create, experience, share, and allow as much joy as you possibly can.

Now that you know, are you ready to accept it?

ON: OPINIONS

You know, Dear One, it isn't absolutely necessary for you to express your opinion about everything.

It's okay to reserve doing so for only those things that you agree with or feel hopeful about, that lift your spirits and that hold promise for you, that you find beauty in and that make you feel good, regardless of how much others may try to convince you otherwise.

That does not mean that we are encouraging you to turn a blind eye to all that you find unjust or heartbreaking in the world.

It simply means that, throughout the history of time, pouring negatively charged words, actions, or feeling into a situation that is distressing, troublesome, harmful, or toxic has never, not ever, not even once, solved it.

ON: WHY BE YOURSELF?

Why are we always encouraging you to follow your heart, be yourself, and stop trying to be the person you think you should be, or the one that you think the world wants you to be?

When you think, act, speak, and behave authentically, genuinely, and from your heart, Dear One, you and your words, actions, and thoughts are infinitely more powerful, interesting, fun, lovable, accessible, desirable, attractive—more everything—than any illusion of you ever could be.

ON: ACHIEVING MASTERY

Mastery is not about perfection, Dear One, or doing, being, or creating something that is the best, or better than anyone else.

To achieve mastery is to achieve a state of being fully present, fully aware of what is happening around you and within you, and what is available to you in each and every unique moment of your life, acknowledging it, taking it in, allowing it to inspire, inform, motivate, shape, and influence your thoughts, actions, and beliefs from moment to moment.

Masters are not superior beings, Dear One. They are not better people than everyone else. They are simply more practiced at living in the now and taking advantage of all the gifts that are available to them in the present moment.

They don't try to create exceptional, superior, or richer work, but being fully present, they have a deeper, richer, more connected, productive, and fruitful experience of each moment, and that experience is expressed in and translated into all they do.

If you want to achieve mastery, Dear One, don't try to be better at what you do; try to be more present while you are doing it, and you will be on your way.

ON: THE POWER OF CREATIVITY

Creativity is one of the most powerful tools at your disposal, Dear One. It can turn an old tire into a swing, flour into bread, a stone into a gem, a piece of paper into a poem, an empty space into a home, a dream into reality.

Your life is not lacking opportunity, Dear One, only a little imagination.

ON: GIVING VS. TAKING

Be generous, Dear One, with your spirit, your gifts, your heart, in all that you do.

There is no reason for you to hold back. You will never run out of any of the wonderful qualities that make you who you are. In fact, the more of yourself that you give away, the quicker you will find yourself restored. Share your gifts, share yourself. Allow both to flow freely out into the world.

Remember, Dear One, you live in an abundant universe where there is no lack.

But know that there is a big difference between giving of yourself and having others take from you. You will know the difference by how it feels, because one is restorative and energizing and the other is draining. Take notice of how your energy is flowing from you, through you, out into the world.

Once you become aware of the difference between giving your energy willingly and having it taken from you, either aggressively or passively, it is our belief that you will at once acquire an awareness of how to protect yourself and prevent the latter from taking place.

Once you learn to see and direct how and where your energy flows, no one and nothing will ever be able to take it from you again without your consent.

ON: WHY FORGIVE?

Forgive them for their mistakes, Dear One.

Forgive their shortcomings, faults, ignorance, and impatience. Forgive their actions when they react out of fear, their words when they respond from pain, their behavior when they get defensive, and their callousness when they are cruel.

They are not perfect. They are deeply flawed. They are hurting, healing, learning, and coping the best way they know. Believe it or not, they are actually doing the very best that they believe themselves to be capable of.

They are imperfect, Dear One—just like you.

Forgive them without expectation, condition, or question and without hesitation. Why? Because doing so is one of the most powerful gifts of self-love, acceptance, and forgiveness you can give to yourself.

ON: EVEN-STEVEN

There are no levels, Dear One, when it comes to the value of human life. No one life is more or less valuable than any other. You are not more or less than anyone, and they are not more or less than you. Whether or not you (or they) choose to believe it and acknowledge it, you are all of equal value in the eyes of spirit.

The greatest measure of differentiation between you all, Dear One, is the way in which you choose to value and respect each other, and yourselves.

ON: WHY LOVE ONE ANOTHER?

Why should you reach out, open yourself up, be vulnerable, risk rejection, take a chance, cross boundaries, follow your heart, say what you feel, and connect, Dear One?

The answer is simple—because it feels so good to do so.

ON: THE IMPORTANCE OF SELF-CARE

Never feel guilty about taking care of yourself, Dear One.

Never feel bad about putting yourself first, regardless of what anyone else has to say about it. Not only is it necessary for you to do so, but also we are counting on you to do a lot more of it.

Those who give you a hard time about looking after yourself don't yet understand how vitally important it is for you, for your health and happiness, and for your ability to help them and to have something of value to offer the rest of the world.

Someone's got to teach them, Dear One.

Someone's got to show them how it is done.

Why not you?

CHAPTER 8: A LESSON ON LISTENING

How can you learn to hear us on your own?

Asking us to teach you how to hear us on your own, Dear One, is a little like asking us to teach you how to hear a dog bark, or a bell ring, or a train whistle blow. It is just not something we can do. When all the parts of your anatomy that are required for perceiving sound are functioning properly, your ears just work, and you can hear. It is not something that you can or need to be taught. It is simply something that you can do.

Hearing us works in much the same way. When your energetic anatomy is working, and all the pieces of your spiritual self are functioning properly, you can hear us. Pay attention and there we are!

But your ability to hear us is not the problem, Dear One—that is not the reason why you do not. Everyone, and yes, we do mean everyone, has the ability to hear, feel, connect, and talk directly with spirit any time they like. You have been able to do that since the moment you arrived in this physical realm and you will be able to do so until the moment you depart. By virtue of the fact that you have a soul, that you are a soul, a divine spirit, you have all of the energetic anatomy that is required.

Listening, accepting, and believing that you can is the challenge you are up against.

It's not that you can't hear us, Dear One, it is simply that you don't believe you can. So what can we do about that? How can we get you over this hurdle? How can we help you listen, accept, and believe? Well, the short answer is, we can't.

There is nothing we can do for you, Dear One, but there is a lot you can do for yourself. And the first step you need to take is to change the way you listen and what you are listening for. You have to be willing to listen, knowing that words, wisdom, guidance, and support are being directed toward you, waiting to be heard, at all times.

When you take a breath, Dear One, you know that air is going to fill your lungs, do you not? You do not question each breath, wondering or doubting whether oxygen will be available to you. You trust in it, allow it, confidently rely on it. Breathing is an act of knowing, Dear One, an act of trusting. Can you see that?

We would like you to think about connecting with spirit, listening to and hearing us in much the same way. We are here, Dear One. We are talking to you, always. We are reaching out to you, always. We are guiding you, always, always, always.

Breathe us in, listen for us, look for our guidance, love, and support, trust it, know that it is there as confidently as you know that the air you need will be there when you take your next breath. You trust that each breath you take will deliver to you exactly what you need. We would like you to trust that so, too, will listening to spirit.

Hearing is not an act of trying, Dear One; it is an act of knowing.

A PLACE TO CONNECT

What do you want to know, Dear One? Tell us what your questions are. Ask us anything you like. And then quiet your mind, open your heart, and listen. Use these pages to write down the answers that you know we are sharing with you.

"Connect with your heart, listen to what it has to say, and allow it to guide you."

"Look. Listen. Feel. Trust. We are here,
Dear One. Always."

"You are living a life surrounded by spirit."

"Open up wider, make room for something new, create space for something different."

"Everyone has the ability to hear and connect with spirit."

"Trust that the answer will come to you, allow it to, and it will!"

_____

_____

_____

_____

_____

_____

_____

_____

_____

_____

_____

_____

_____

_____

_____

_____

_____

_____

_____

"Know, Dear One, that you are most definitely not in this alone."

CLOSING

It is with our most sincere and eternal gratitude, Dear One, that we say thank you...

• for being a good friend

• for loving them as only you can

• for forgiving, letting go, and allowing yourself to heal

• for taking a risk, being brave, and speaking up

• for telling the truth, revealing yourself, and sharing your story

• for doing something that you have never done before

• for going somewhere that you have never gone before

• for using your life to create

• for every moment that you choose to live with an open heart and an open mind

We are all better off because of it, because of you.

ACKNOWLEDGMENTS

I started writing this book long before I knew I was even writing a book. My guides, my champions, my constant companions in this life, told me so every day as I diligently penned the messages they were sharing with me over the past three years. But as I did with so much of the wisdom they imparted to me back then, I completely disregarded it. "Who am I, after all, to do something so grand as to write a book?" I would ask. "An author," they replied.

In writing this book I have actually felt more like a reporter than an author, as nearly all of the content has been dictated to me and not written by me. As I was nearing the end of this process and all the pieces were falling into place, I asked my guides how I could possibly put my name on something that was so clearly not my own. They told me that no one does anything in this life by themselves and that just because an experience is shared does not make it any less mine. And I chose to believe them.

There are so many people who shared in the experience of writing this book with me, and it is my hope that they all feel just as connected, proud, and responsible for the content as I do. They all played a major role in successfully elevating either me or the content, or both, over the past year. Without every word, hug, nudge, shove, and kick in the pants I received from them, all of this would never have come to pass.

I would like to acknowledge and express my gratitude to them all for their tremendous and constant support, patience, love, candor, persistence, and contribution to this project and to my life. If it were up to me, all our names would be on the cover.

Daniele Berna	Paul Lynch
Carmel Edmonds	Cate Parsons
Anthony Giovanniello	Kristine Pidkameny
Jan Guarino	Cindy Richards
Joe Komljenovich	Amanda Stevens
Florence Kusnetz	Bob Thomas
William Lee	Fara Levy Yarbrough

Thank you to each and every one of you for sharing yourself, your gifts, and your lives with me. It has been my great pleasure, honor, and joy co-creating with you all.

Michelle